# Instagram Marketing 2023

How to Find Your Dream
Clients, Build a Community of
Raving Fans, and Catapult Your
Business in Just 7 Steps

**Wayne Peters**

from various sources. Please consult a licensed professional before attempting any techniques outlined in this book.

By reading this document, the reader agrees that under no circumstances is the author responsible for any losses, direct or indirect, that are incurred as a result of the use of the information contained within this document, including, but not limited to, errors, omissions, or inaccuracies.

# Table of Contents

# Step 1:

# Getting Started

Social media has changed the way customers interact with brands and how brands interact with their customers. Brand-to-customer relations are skyrocketing as brands can have genuine one-on-one conversations and feedback from their customers, of which they use to elevate their brands. Customers are also given the opportunity to feel that their opinions matter regarding their favorite brands, and the opportunity to influence change.

What was once considered a platform for keeping up with friends and family has now grown into the e-commerce space. You can sell, interact one-on-one with customers, and make short announcements or run ads about anything new in your company without breaking the bank.

Social media platforms like Instagram have become so powerful in the customer journey that customers will first interact with a company's social media profile before making a buying decision. As a business owner, you need to optimize and utilize the opportunity provided by social media sites to meet consumer demands.

Instagram has different account types tailored to different needs, i.e., personal, business, and creator. The basic features on Instagram remain the same across the whole platform. Still, additional features and tools are available for the profile types available for content creators, professionals looking to create an online brand, public figures, and business owners. These are the business and content creator account types. These accounts enable businesses and influencers to stand out with useful, additional features designed to help them utilize the platform maximumly.

Deciding what account you want all goes back to what your objectives are from having a presence on Instagram in the first place. But before you choose which account to set up your brand, ask yourself, *is Instagram the right place for my product or service*? Even more importantly, who is your target customer, and how likely are they to use Instagram daily? Understanding this step is essential because it will allow you to define the rest of the process and optimize your business messages for your customers. You wouldn't want to sell something meant for a particular audience to the general public that doesn't have daily use or interest in it.

# Creator Versus Business Accounts

Instagram's creator and business accounts are designed for those looking for a little more resources to help them use Instagram strategically, like learning about their audience, the audience behaviors, buying habits, etc. You can choose between a business account or a creator account, depending on the type of business you are running or the service provided; but which one is best for you?

**Creator Account:**

According to Instagram, creator accounts are best suited for public figures, content creators, photographers, artists, and influencers. Creator accounts were rolled out fairly recently and enable any user who wants to switch from a personal account to a creator account to do so with great ease. You can switch to this account type regardless of the number of followers, which wasn't the case before. Using a creator account acts as a portfolio for creatives.

Pros:

- Creator Studio that helps track page growth and post performance via desktop

- can include shoppable content in posts

- arranging your inbox into three categories for eased management, with a customized FAQ

- option to have your page appear as a regular page or a business page (with contact details and category details on display or not)

- post scheduling options via Creator Studio

Cons:

- Creator Studio only showcases past seven days' worth of insights

- limited monetization options

- limited scheduling functions

- page can't be set as private

**Business Account:**

Instagram business accounts are recommended for retailers, local businesses, brands, organizations, or service providers. Your business profile acts as a social website that introduces your audience to your product or service in action before they get to decide if they want to use it or not. Business accounts provide slightly different features from creator accounts.

Pros:

- access to important analytics and insights for your page and business impact

- access Instagram shops by linking your shop to Instagram or creating a catalog

- customized FAQs for direct messages

- customized call to action buttons like visit website, book a demo, and make a reservation

- branded content tools

- can link your Facebook and Instagram pages and enable cross-posting

Cons:

- You can't add links to Stories unless verified or have 10,000+ followers.

- You can't make your page private.

Initially, both Creator and Business profiles offer users almost the same features and benefits, but it goes back to what is important to you and your brand. This will help you determine which one of the two options to choose from, considering that Instagram recommends the two different accounts for different types of users. Instagram, however, allows for easy switching between all their account types, so you can play around back and forth to find which one you prefer using based on its delivery of your needs.

## *Instagram Content Types*

Instagram has four kinds of content types you can post on your feed: Post, Story, Reel, and Live.

## Posts

Instagram posts can be images or videos. That is the traditional way people interact with Instagram. When someone explores your page, they are the dominant content type and appear first out of all your content types. Those little squares of content allow you to create compelling images or share videos with your audience about anything you wish. They can also be posted in the form of a carousel, where you post a series of 2 to 10 images or videos under a single post.

## Reels

Instagram Reels are short, creative videos brands use to bring their brand content to life or add a touch of humanity to make them more relatable and authentic to their audience. They are a fun way to jump on trends, interact with your audience, and play around with your brand in a fun and creative way. Reels run anywhere between 15 seconds to 60 seconds.

## Stories

Stories are posts that last for precisely 24 hours before they expire. They are a great way to interact one-on-one with your audience, build anticipation, and give a glimpse into the daily activities of your brand. Many brands use Instagram Stories to keep their audience updated on any kind of information they wish to share without necessarily having it on their page grid. If you want to keep your Stories longer and active on your page, you can use the Highlights feature, where they will show up indefinitely at the top of your profile right before your posts.

## *Videos*

Unlike carousel videos or Reels, videos can run for longer than 60 seconds. They can go to a maximum of 10 minutes or 60 minutes for select accounts. Videos can be posted separately or as part of a carousel, which plays only the first 60 seconds of the video. Your audience will then have to scroll through the carousel to watch the rest of the posted video. They are suitable for posting long-form, educational content that adds value to your audience. Because it's longer, you want to give them something they will be interested in to keep watching beyond the first 60 seconds.

**Step 2:**

# Understanding the

# Instagram Algorithms

The Instagram algorithms are a set of rules that define which posted content is prioritized based on a set of different factors. They have the power to make or break your content, which makes it a very powerful tool that you as a business owner on Instagram need to constantly keep up with. The algorithms decide which posts show up on a user's feed and the order they are featured, which posts show up under their Explore page, and which Stories show up first on their Stories panel.

Instagram recently rolled out some new features in how users can personalize their Instagram feed in two different ways, different from the default feed:

- Following: The following feed sorts your feed to showcase chronologically posts from accounts you follow, starting from most recently posted.

- Favorites: This sorts your feed into only handles you marked as favorites. Any other accounts, regardless if you follow them or not, don't show up if it's not manually added to your favorites account list.

The default page view, also known as Home, is determined by user interests and how often someone interacts with certain accounts or contents. The algorithms determine for a user what posts to view in this case, as opposed to the Following and Favorites options in which the user has more control. The Home feed does not have a chronological option like the other two. Posts can be recent or as far back as a week and longer.

## Factors That Affect Your Ranking

There are base factors that determine what users see or don't see based on what kind of content users like, share, save, or comment on. The Instagram algorithms then work to show them more of this content. There are, however, other factors that determine what will help you rank higher on your followers' feeds, or get discovered by new people.

- Posting frequency: Instagram algorithms favor accounts that post frequently and are active over those that aren't. While the recommended balance is about two to three posts per week, there are other ways you can actively keep on top of your followers' lists without necessarily spamming their feeds. You can use Stories and Reels to break up your content into different content types. This ensures you stay active without necessarily spamming your followers with numerous posts. The beauty of Stories is that you can post as many or as little as you want without spamming anyone because it's much faster to swipe to the next account on Stories.

- Engagement frequency: Engagement is between you and your followers, and your followers with your content. Your posts are likely to show up more on your follower's feed when they engage with you or your content often enough. Engagement is in terms of how often they like, comment, or share your posts. It is also how often you interact with your followers. The more actively engaged you are, the more likely you'll be recommended to other users with similar app habits as the followers you engage with.

- Relevance of your posts: Instagram algorithms ensure that the users of the platform get what it is they want to see and interact with. It does this by understanding the kind of content that users interact with most, then curating and grouping it for them on their feed, but especially the Explore tab for discovering new accounts. If a user follows and interacts a lot with beauty brands, then their feed and Explore page will make it so they have easy access to beauty-related content. The chance of your content showing up on someone's screen is determined by how often they interact with brands in your niche.

- Relationship with the user: Do you follow each other? Do they follow you? What is the history with you and that follower in terms of their frequency in commenting or liking your posts? Do they visit your page? All these are high determinants of when and how often you'll show up in front of your followers. If your content pushes a follower to take action, you are more likely to show up higher on their feed or on the Explore page for users with a similar interest.

- Type of content: Some users interact more with videos, while others interact more with images. The algorithms enable a user to find their preferences much faster, which makes it more likely for your followers to find your content faster (or not). When creating your Instagram content strategy, it is important that you include all content types in your plan to be able to cater to different user preferences.

For every post you make the major determinants of its expansion to numerous people are the following:

- likes

- comments

- shares

- saves

These are big indicators to the algorithm that your content is interesting enough to warrant action from their users, so your content will be given priority. The faster people take action, the higher you'll be able to rank and show up to people with similar habits as those interacting with your content.

## *Tips to Rank Higher*

1. Post frequently

Posting frequency is important because the algorithms give priority to the latest posts. And with the rollout of the customized Favorites and Following feeds, it's become even more important to keep up your posting frequency to ensure your engagement levels don't drastically drop and affect your marketing efforts. While you shouldn't post content that turns into spam, you also shouldn't do it so infrequently that your page gets drowned out, like posting only once or twice a whole month.

2. Post relevant content

If your brand is a lifestyle brand, it makes no sense to have content talking about NFTs or cryptocurrency. The people that follow you do so because they are attracted to your content, and creating posts that are not related in any way in terms of content matter or niche creates a disconnected feed, which leads to limited engagement with your content, or even getting unfollowed. There is a lot to be posted under a lifestyle niche; find out what it is, and keep it relevant.

3. Create shareable content

If numerous people, those who follow you and those who don't, share your content, or interact enough with your content, the possibility of having your posts show up in front of more people gets higher. If you want to know what kind of content gets shared the most and the kind of messages in that content, you can check out your Explore feed to learn more about what's being shared, especially in your niche. Shareable content is relatable, funny, or inspiring enough for someone to want to show the same message to others or to keep it to come back to at some point.

4. Engage your community

Stories are a great way to start conversations, encourage contests, and gather opinions by using the numerous available stickers to your advantage. You can also look at having a strong call to action included in your captions for every post to help you control and drive conversations with your community.

5.  Use the features available

Instagram has interactive features that you can use to your advantage to help you drive engagement and push you higher on the rankings. You can play around with stickers for Stories, trending audios for Reels, long-form videos, creating content within trending and relevant hashtags, etc.

6.  Study the insights

Instagram provides insights that enable you to study your audience's behavior. This helps you find the optimal way to interact with your following and use the app to grow or strategize for maximum benefit.

**Step 3:**

# Creating a Winning

# Strategy

Marketing of any kind starts with creating a marketing strategy. A well-defined marketing strategy is crucial because it provides a clear outline of the work you have to get done. It also clarifies what to post when, so your content doesn't look random, rushed, or disconnected. Marketing strategies for any company need to capture the brand voice and showcase what you stand for and what you believe in giving you a competitive edge because your content speaks for you when you can't. So before you get started posting, work on your content strategy for Instagram.

But how?

A marketing or content strategy fundamentally seeks to define who you are, what you do, how you will benefit your customers, and what you want from your customers. Who you are defines what you stand for as a business or influencer and your personality. This is usually the first thing that a customer will notice about you. What you do seeks to define your services or products, which will be what attracts a customer to your page in the first place. What you can do for them explains how your specific product or service will benefit the customer or help them make a buying decision. What you want from your customers translates into the goals you set for creating the content strategy in the first place. Do you want to have more followers? Do you want to generate more leads? Increase brand engagement?

Designing a marketing strategy will save you time and ideally help you have a more organized schedule, beautifully crafted messages, and a flowing content page. Your audience will always know if and when you are randomly posting because posts made randomly almost always have a significant disconnect from the other posts. It will especially be glaringly obvious if you set a certain standard for yourself that your audience keeps you to.

# Step-By-Step Guide to Creating a Content Strategy

## Step 1: Defining the End Goal

What is a house without its blueprints? What is a plan without a vision? To fulfill something, one needs to understand what one wants to achieve. To create a winning content strategy, you need first to understand and define the end goal, i.e., what you want from your customers, and why you are marketing on Instagram in the first place. The end goal informs about 80% of your marketing strategy by informing you what you need to plan for and where your focus needs to be. When you have the end goal in mind, you can plan how to best achieve it.

To define what your end goal is, ask yourself:

- Why are you creating an Instagram account in the first place?

Maybe you want to find your customers where they are? Or perhaps you are looking to expand your business reach? What is the reason that drove you to create a business account?

- What do you want to achieve, customer-wise?

This will be the end result of the customer journey after they've purchased from you. What does that look like? Is it increased sales, improved conversion rates, or driving traffic to your website?

- What do you want to achieve business-wise?

These are your business objectives. Do you wish to increase company sales by 10% or maybe penetrate new, unexplored markets? Maybe you simply need increased exposure even though no purchases are made?

- Who is your product for, and how likely are they to take it up?

Is it for adults with their own money that can make a buying decision on the spot? Or children who need to convince their parents to buy it for them? Who your product is for means you can design your messages in a way that appeals to them.

## *Step 2: Define the Buyer Persona*

Knowing your customer is as important as knowing your end goal. This is because understanding who your customer is and what their behavior is will help you tailor the exact services and content that they most engage with. Customers are a significant part of your marketing strategy because everything you do is tailored toward fulfilling your company's goals by providing the customer with what they want. You won't want to waste energy and money selling your product or service to people that have no use for it, would you? Ideally, creating more than one buyer persona would be best because no two people are the same when making buying decisions, even with their similarities. To define your buyer persona, ask yourself:

- Who is your ideal customer?

This is who you envision buying from you. It is essential to know who your ideal customer(s) is so you can create content targeted specifically to their needs. For example, someone who likes quality and luxurious products wants to smell or look good and is always looking for something exciting (your service offer defines the ideal customer).

- What are their demographics?

Demographics help you understand what your customers look like. For example, they are young women between 18 and 30, they have a job that pays at least $1,000 per month, and live in a busy city. You can create three or four other demographics to get a thorough idea of what your ideal customers look like. Remember, even if they share similarities and interests, they are still different people that don't all fit in one box.

- What are their buying patterns?

This defines what your customers spend money on, how they buy—like buying in bulk, a couple of products, or one at a time—and where they buy it (is it online or in person?). Buying patterns are useful to know because they can potentially help you define how a customer will access your products, whether they start with buying virtually then receiving physically, or being entirely physical.

- Do they like the trends or not?

Some customers want trendy things, while others prefer unique and tailored products or services. This helps you know if and when you'd have to jump on new trends to keep up with your customers' needs or keep providing customized and unique items to fit their needs. It's also possible to appeal to both kinds of customers, those who like trends and those who prefer unique things. It goes back to how your products can be packaged in a way that both kinds of needs are catered for.

- What kind of content do they interact with the most?

Instagram is not short of content types, and everyone has their favorite. Some people prefer Reels and spend their whole time on Instagram interacting with them. Others interact with Stories more. There are also short-form videos, long-form videos, carousels, etc. Can you identify what kind of content your buyer persona interacts with the most?

- What is their personal life like?

How do they spend their weekends, and where are they most likely to hang out? What are their friends like? Where do they get their news? While this may seem irrelevant, it can help you understand your customer better. For example, as a skincare service provider with customers who take vacations now and then, you could provide solutions for those customers that keep them protected when on the move or ease their skincare routine by providing travel-sized options for your products. Knowing what your customer does for fun also expands your service reach by offering solutions to the problems and challenges they might experience.

- Their values?

People like knowing that their favorite brands care about them, and that starts with understanding what your customer values. Skincare enthusiasts care for cruelty-free products. They care for how you treat your employees because they are the gateway into your company, and most importantly, they care for brands that take a stand for what they believe in. Knowing your customers' values helps you reach out to them in a way that respects or supports what they believe in.

- How often are they online?

Knowing when your ideal customer is online is very important to drive sales as a business looking to sell online. The Instagram chronological feed prioritizes the newest posts. If your followers or ideal customers have this activated, having your post seen when they are online can increase or decrease, depending on when you post and if they are online.

- What do they use Instagram for?

Some people would use Instagram for news, to find trends, or learn something, while others want to keep up with friends and family. Understanding what your customer uses Instagram for enables you to create messages that fit their demands.

## *Step 3: Competitor Analysis*

Your competitors are in the same market as you and probably offer the same product or service. You'll most likely have the same buyer persona, and this is where you will find the people you are looking for. They are also an excellent way to find best practices like customer engagement, marketing strategies, and what to do better by answering or solving your customers' pain points.

- Who are your competitors?

Before running a competitive analysis, you need to know who you are analyzing in the first place. It is best if you ideally look out for both big and small brands because it gives you a general idea of how consumers interact within your niche. Big brands also do things differently from small brands to engage with their customers and receive feedback. It could be a good way to learn something new.

- What kind of content are they using?

Usually, specific industries have certain types of content that work best for driving engagement. A skincare company benefits from making videos about their products and showing their customers how to use them, while a photographer will benefit from photos of their work. You can check out your competitors' pages to understand which content they use the most, how they use it, and what their engagement is.

- What industry hashtags do they use the most?

Hashtags are a way to help the algorithms identify the kind of content in your post and categorize it with similar posts. Many people keep up with hashtags on subjects they are interested in, which means your posts' visibility increases significantly when you include hashtags in them. They go beyond your followers and reach a broader audience that was already looking for something in your industry. Your competitors will be using these hashtags. It's an excellent way to explore which ones are the most popular and the kind of content under those hashtags. This provides a clear picture of what you will be competing with for customer attention.

- What is their customer engagement like?

Some companies post a lot of content, but the engagement isn't there, while others post focused content that translates to engagement. The idea is to notice the patterns between which content gets the most engagement and which is the least engaged. This can also help you identify what your potential customers are most drawn to, so you have a benchmark of what the industry standards are. Overall, engagement helps you rank higher on your followers' homepages, which means you need to understand how and when potential customers are most likely to engage with your industry or niche.

- What are customers saying about them?

Customer feedback is an excellent way to know what things resonate with your customers and what other brands are doing well. This sets the bar for what your minimum expectations will be. It's also helpful to determine how often a given company showcases reviews and user-generated content. These are very important in helping people decide to buy a product when they see someone review or praise your product.

- What is their business model like?

Many companies utilize aspects like influencers and running ads to drive traffic to their pages. Sometimes running ads is more rewarding than influencers, while other times influencers increase a company's reach and engagement more drastically. Knowing your competitor's business model helps you understand the best way to stand out, especially if you are looking to penetrate a new market.

- What makes their brand unique?

Can you find out what about your competition makes them stand out to their customers? People are attracted to things that they find fascinating, and being unique is an excellent way to surprise your customers to want to take up your product. Something as simple as your product/service packaging can attract new customers.

- What is the rate of follower engagement?

To calculate the rate of followers to engagement, you use a simple formula: Add the total number of likes and comments on a post, divide that by the total number of followers and multiply by 100. You can do this for your competitors to get an idea of their engagement average on a given number of posts. An average engagement ratio is between 1% to 3.5%. Higher is even better. The engagement ratio is an excellent way to understand how well content performs outside merely having many followers. The engagement ratio also shows how often your content shows up in front of your followers, and is a good way to judge if your content is quality enough to get prioritized by the algorithms.

## *Step 4: Craft Your Message*

Your message is everything you want your customer to know about you. Even if you know it by heart, it helps to have it written down, especially in instances where you will not be working alone. What you want to be known for is important to avoid people wondering how you changed from one service or product to another. You've probably seen comments like "I thought you sold candles!" or "Since when did you offer (product)?" Comments like this show that your customers or community have no idea precisely what you are saying, mainly because of how you package your message. You want to be able to avoid comments like that. It's also best to craft your message before the content itself because the message will help you align your content within your brand voice.

- Identify your value proposition.

This is a simple summary of why a customer should buy from you. What value will they get when they use your product over another? To identify your value proposition, it's best to know your customers' pain points (from running a buyer persona) and specifically identify how your product will solve this problem. It is short, straight to the point, and immediately sells your services or product to a potential buyer.

- Identify your content pillars.

These can be three to six blocks of your main brand themes that tell your story as a brand. You will use these pillars to tell your brand's story through images, carousels, Reels, and Stories. Having your content pillars also comes in handy later when you start creating posts, so you know what kind of subjects need to be in your posts. Examples of content pillars for a travel company could be tips on travel, accommodation, and places of interest. Depending on whether you are a company that promotes travel or a travel blogger, there is a lot you can explore and talk about using these three content pillars.

- What is your brand identity/esthetic?

Some have particular hashtags; others have specific colors, items, or brand themes. You want something that immediately stands out, and people can relate to you as soon as they see it. For example, the apple with a side piece missing is a unique symbol that everyone refers directly to the Apple Inc. brand, or the Instagram colors, which you can immediately connect to Instagram.

- How will you convince your customer to contribute to your end goal?

Generally, a call to action is an excellent way to convince someone to take up your product, but a call to action is preceded by a great caption or content in the post. That is why you need your content pillars, as they will guide a consumer on what you do and what you want them to do about this. It is also a good idea to brainstorm what kind of messages you'd like to convey for every post you make, whether you want to end or start with the same point, etc.

## *Step 5: Creating a Content Calendar*

Your research and all the other steps we just went through boil down to this last step: creating a content calendar. This will guide you in knowing what to post when, so you don't randomly wake up and post something that doesn't align. Content calendars are generally used to help you keep track of what you need to post or what was posted, and are an excellent way to track your performance and help you get organized.

- Break down your content pillars.

Your content pillars are generally what your business is all about, so you'd need to break them down to find something you can post that falls under the different pillars. These are called "content ideas." Going by the travel example in the previous step, you can break down the "Places of Interest" content pillar into ideas like a beach you loved, a restaurant you would recommend, a must-see local attraction, etc. These ideas are what you will be basing your creation of posts on. You can break down an idea further by giving value to your post using the "Educate, Entertain, Excite" formula. For an idea like "A must-see local attraction," you can post a historical fact about it you feel people should know or tell an entertaining or inspiring story (maybe about a local you met, etc.). This helps you optimize your content and have a clear idea of your call to action. You can also incorporate "theme days" that give your customers something to look forward to every week. Maybe Thursday becomes #TipThursday, where all your posts are about giving your followers tips that go beyond using your product or service but are still within your niche.

- How often would you be posting?

Some people go for it once a day for five days a week; others go for it three times a week, and some post different kinds of content daily (photos, Reels, Stories). It all goes back to what type of information you post and the engagement level. Generally, even your industry itself matters. Someone in the journalism industry is expected to keep their followers up-to-date, and when anything happens, their loyal followers will automatically check out their page first. On the other hand, someone selling a business or service can overwhelm their customers if they see your posts marketing your product every two or three posts. By posting Stories or Reels or mixing them up now and then, you can use the different content to keep you in front of your customers without overwhelming them.

- What resources and management tools will you be using?

There are a lot of social media management tools that you can use to help you manage and schedule your content. Others will help you create this content. Websites like Later, Buffer, and Hootsuite provide you with options to schedule your content ahead of time and manage analytics. Suppose you have your Instagram account connected to a Facebook page. In that case, you can use the Facebook Business Suite to schedule and post on both your Facebook and Instagram accounts and manage the pages without going back and forth between the two accounts. Tools like Canva or Photoshop, on the other hand, will help you create your content.

- What should your content calendar have?

An effective content calendar clearly defines the date, time, content type, caption, hashtags, and the content itself. You want to have a calendar where you will copy and paste content, and defining all this helps you optimize your time by merely posting or scheduling your content. It is an effective way to stay organized and keep you up to par with what you'll be posting. The beauty about having a content calendar is that you have all your posts created and ready to be posted ahead of time, so when it comes time to schedule or post, you don't have to spend extra time coming up with a caption or thinking about hashtags.

- Keep up with trends.

Trends and viral videos or challenges come and go. They always have many people jumping on them or scrolling endlessly, making it an excellent way to gain brand visibility and increase engagement. However, the thing about trends is that not everything will fall under your niche–in fact, almost all trends never fall under a specific niche–but that doesn't mean you can't use the trend. Instagram Reels provide you an opportunity to remix a sound. You can use a viral sound totally unrelated to what you are doing or trying to sell and then make it authentically yours and entertaining. This is something to keep in mind when creating your content calendar. Trends and viral moments come randomly, so be ready to create something around that trend if it makes sense for your brand to join.

**Step 4:**

# Finding Your Community

A community on Instagram transcends more than just having followers. While you want to gain brand visibility through numerous new followers, building a community is more rewarding. Followers are likely to occasionally and passively interact with your content. On the other hand, a community is always actively engaged, resharing/reposting your content, tagging friends, or saving posts, all of which work in helping you rank higher according to the Instagram algorithms. A community is literally who is going to stand by you and support your product beyond merely commenting and liking your posts.

Building a community is a never-ending process and keeps changing the more brand visibility you gain. This process requires you to look for your community where it is, which means there will be a lot of "putting yourself out there," especially if you are a new brand trying to gain visibility among your potential clients and preferred niche. Some might find this uncomfortable to do, but it is inevitable. The whole idea behind building a community is to boost brand loyalty as the number one go-to for anything niche-related among your followers and stay in front of your customers. This kind of thing demands your time, sacrifice, and maybe even some tears.

Building a community should not be confused with growing your follower count. The number of Instagram account followers is crucial because it's a great indicator of brand visibility. Still, you should also consider how to grow with the followers you already have and build stronger personal relationships with them.

This is what you should consider as you create a plan to build your community:

- What more value can you create for the followers you already have? If you can't give value to the 100 followers you have now, chances are, you won't provide value to the 1000 followers you want to gain.

- What is important to your customers? Customers let you know what is important to them through comments on a product or reviews they leave on the medium they access your product. It is important to listen to your audience because they communicate precisely what they want/wish to have.

- What can you provide of value to your customer according to what is important to them? Knowing this will help you understand exactly how to craft your messages to fit your customer's needs, and get you on the road to building a community.

How to Build a Community:

- Keep it personal.

You might be a brand, but behind that brand is a person first. That is what you want your followers to associate you with beyond being simply a brand, because it's much easier to relate to a person than it is to something that isn't living and breathing. Numerous consumers like the connection they feel to a person and are readily willing to purchase from the people that they admire. Being personal does not mean sharing your life story, however. Far from that, actually. It can be as simple as finding a name for your online community that sets you apart from others or immediately identifies who relates to your brand. Celebrities like Beyonce have the Beyhive and Rihanna with the Navy. Their communities identify each other with these names, and those who identify as being a part of that community will readily back up the person they believe in. While you can't always address every individual in your community by name, calling them by a name they all identify with is a great way to make people feel like you are personally addressing them as long as they identify as a part of your community. Find tasteful ways to keep it personal by creating content that your followers find thought-provoking, are excited to engage with, and are willing to share because it says something to them. Break down the barrier between you and your followers by being personal in how you communicate, so people remember that behind this post is an actual human who cares about the things they care about.

- Stay authentic.

Social media is generally a competitive place where everyone tries to one-up the other, especially on Instagram. All you have to show for what you are up to is through heavily edited photos. Users find authentic content a breath of fresh air, so as a content creator or someone looking at starting, you shouldn't be worried about what people like more than what more you can give to them. The disconnect sometimes happens when what you are selling or what you represent as a brand targets a specific group of people versus having something for numerous people. An example is high-end fashion brands whose clothes are only affordable to a particular income bracket versus brands that have clothes that fit within all economic brackets. Users also like knowing that you are real and your products do what you say they do. If you are a shapewear brand, it makes no sense to photoshop a picture to distort the real effects when your customer uses your product, or use heavy filters to distort the reality of what your skincare products can or can't do. Be authentic by showing the truth behind every picture you post, whether it's the numerous struggles you faced trying on the product, or behind the scenes of that glamorous photo you posted a few days ago. The idea is to not alienate your following, by reminding them that you, too, have bad days as much as you have good days, and have leeway to connect with them on a personal level.

- Engage with your followers.

Instagram provides a plethora of tools to create engaging content for your following. However, the best way to build a community is through using features like Instagram Live, which provides you an opportunity to have one-on-one conversations with your followers in real time and grow meaningful relationships. Lives also put you at the number one spot on Instagram Stories, which is a great way to gain visibility among your followers and community. You can also encourage your followers to reach out to you if they have any questions about your product and how to use it. You can do this by including a call to action at the end of every post made that is aligned to driving sales or simply talking about your product or service. You can also encourage people to use a hashtag specific to your brand/product or tag you whenever they use your product or service and ask permission to repost their reviews. This is a great way to encourage others to engage with your content, consume your product or service, and talk about it. New followers or potential consumers always want to know what others already using your product or service have to say about it. This makes it easy for them to make a buying decision or keep coming back when they receive the value you promised. It's also important that you learn to keep the conversation going and don't make your followers feel like they were left hanging by a comment you didn't answer or an opinion you discouraged. Another great way to create an engaging comment section is by asking a question that gets your comment section alight.

- Work with the algorithms.

Naturally, the people we interact with the most stay on top of our pages on Instagram versus people we rarely interact with. The best way to work with the algorithms is to ensure you interact with and connect with your followers to stay on top of their list. There are numerous ways to do this on Instagram beyond your engaging posts. You can utilize the Stories feature to keep the conversation flowing between you and your followers by creating Stories that will get them reacting, like creating polls to ask for their opinions, interactive Stories that allow your followers to ask you questions, or anything similar that will start a conversation. It doesn't stop there, however; someone responding to your Stories is an invitation to keep the conversation moving with them, which encourages them to keep checking out your Stories if they enjoy your conversations. Go the extra mile by returning the favor and commenting on their posts or Stories to keep it lively, so the conversation doesn't appear one-sided. Another way to keep the conversation moving and using the algorithms is utilizing hashtags to put you where your potential community and followers are. Of course, it all goes back to the kind of quality content you share.

- Collaborate with other creators.

Never underestimate the power of collaboration. When you collaborate with someone within your industry, niche, or who has the same values as you and what you stand for, you open up doors to reach out to an even wider audience through the person you are collaborating with. Before you decide who to collaborate with, you need to ensure that the person you want to work with won't compromise the integrity of your already existing audience or have a negative impact, because these kinds of things are important to your consumers. When you've done your research, understand what each party will be contributing to in the collaboration and what each of you will gain for it to be something of value for both of you. You can also decide how to collaborate, possibly by doing a joint Live session, a Reel, or posting a photo aimed at getting the result of what both parties are looking for.

- Put the work in.

Your brand can only work if you put in the work needed to get you off the ground and running. You can't grow a community without being involved with your community, in your niche, or on your page. The work comes in by creating content, posting the content, interacting with others in your niche, and generally creating a space you want your community to fill. One thing that you should never focus on or have as a strategy to grow is through self-promoting unnecessarily in Instagram comments of people that actually put in the work to produce quality content their followers want: for example, spamming with follow-for-follow comments or trying to declare your expertise in a given subject when none of it reflects on your business pages. Many followers, especially those you are looking at adding to your community, find this kind of self-promotion off-putting and are more likely to block you because you don't add any value to the subject at hand with the comments you leave. Focus your energy on creating shareable content instead, leaving insightful comments that drive people to check out your page, and placing yourself as an expert in a given niche by showcasing that, both on your business page and the comments section of the posts you decide to comment on. This will give people the opportunity to provide you with a genuine follow when you create something that they want to interact with and react to.

- Create impact.

We all like getting information that we can learn from, so why not give value to your audience? Impactful content stays with us because we can use whatever information we receive or simply store it to use for a later date. You can give your audience something they will still use when they put their phone down because that will likely make them return for more. A skincare company can teach its audience how to buy the perfect products for their skin types without necessarily selling its brand. Just providing guidelines to people trying to start their skincare journey or those looking at switching up creates enough impact to have someone want to come back for more. A travel company could give tips about making the most of your stay in a given place by providing information about receiving coupons, discounts, or such practical knowledge your followers can use without being promotional. This kind of advice is invaluable and will occasionally have your audience come back for more, putting you as a trusted source for the important niche-related information they might be looking for.

# The Importance of User-Generated Content

User-generated content (UGC) refers to any content about a brand that the consumers of that brand post. Most consumers look at the experience of already existing customers before they make a buying decision, which makes UGC a very powerful tool. Probably more than any kind of traditional advertising. UGC comes in the form of photos, videos, reviews, and any other such format designed to bring credibility to a brand through its users.

With too many brands offering basically the same product or service, it is easy for a consumer to get overwhelmed by the numerous choices. Peer-reviewed content, however, makes it easy for them to choose one product or service over another. This is because peer reviews are a lot more personal, provide real-life experiences on using a given brand, and are more trusted because a reviewer usually has no incentive to lie about their experience with a product or service. Instagram guidelines also ask for anyone running a sponsorship to indicate so on top of a post, which makes it easy to differentiate between unbiased UGC and paid UGC.

There are two different kinds of user-generated content:

1.  Organic: This refers to social media content made by your community about your product without you necessarily having a say in what they say or how they represent your brand. Organic user-generated content is authentic and can reflect positively or negatively on your brand. Because you have no control over this kind of UGC, it mainly has the most power to drive buying decisions.

2.  Cultivated: This kind of user-generated content is obtained through collaborations with experts in your industry, nano, micro, macro, and mega influencers (depending on your brand needs), and collaborations with like minded brands. Cultivated UGC mainly drives brand visibility more than it drives buying decisions.

Both of these kinds of UGC can be found and used in a different way to drive your online objectives:

**Organic User-Generated Content**

How to find and use:

Your community is most likely to post about your product or service if they are fully engaged with your content.

1. Use your community: They are the most engaged with your brand, which means they will most likely share it. A fully engaged community will understand which hashtags to use to keep your content within your eyesight. They reach out to tell you about their experience with your brand even without prompt at times and are more likely to be excited to send you reviews whenever you ask when they feel you love engaging with them. This, of course, all goes back to how you treat your community, the kind of relationships you foster between each other, and how you interact within your community.

2. Create captions that compel action: Ending your captions with something as simple as "Let me know what you think in the comments section!" or "What has been your experience so far?" is a good way to prompt people to get talking and provide feedback and reviews where potential customers or potential followers would see them. Carefully take time when creating your content calendar to formulate converting captions.

3. Encourage your community to share their experiences: Beyond asking for their opinions, you want to encourage your community to tag you in posts of them using your product or

create a repost prompt where you ask them to tag you so you can repost on your page. This is something that many find compelling and will be more than willing to take pictures of themselves using your product or service for a chance to be featured on your page. You can do this by running a centralized campaign by using hashtags on each post posted or giving rewards according to the given criteria you chose.

4. Create space for feedback: Be willing to let people express themselves, whether negatively or positively. Creating a space for feedback lets a consumer know that they can count on you to listen to what they have to say without it turning into something unpleasant for both parties. Of course, you shouldn't stand for slander just for the sake of receiving feedback. You might also find that some consumers might be entitled, but as a brand, it's your responsibility to de-escalate any situation as positively as you can while remaining firm to what you stand for as a person and brand.

5. Make the content shoppable: Brands that sell products do this best. If you get a chance to feature someone using your brand products on your page, make it shoppable in order to encourage other users to find the exact same pieces. Make sure to remove the guesswork for

your followers by easing how they access information as much as possible. You can set this up through Instagram Shops, which allows you to create a catalog of your products.

## Cultivated User-Generated Content

This kind of content is usually more strategic and aims to serve a purpose between the involved parties. It is mostly driven by public figures and influencers.

1. Create your objectives: The number one thing to consider when looking at creating cultivated UGC is deciding what you want to gain at the end by using this kind of strategy. This is important because your objectives define for you who you choose to go with and what they can contribute to your brand. Do you want brand visibility? A wider reach? Increased sales? To grow brand credibility? It's important to understand what objective you want before spending time and resources on this type of UGC.

2. Decide who you want to work with: Will it be a public figure, influencer, or a similar brand? Public figures don't usually appeal to every consumer bracket, and neither do influencers. If you want to achieve a higher reach, you decide who you want to work with depending on how publicly influential they are, especially towards

your target audience. If you wish to find a small, cozy community to penetrate, chances are you'll find this through influencers and similar brands and not public figures who might have a more generic following. Keep it aligned to your objectives when deciding who to work with, finding the best way both parties might maximize the partnership. It's also important to find out their insights because you need to know their influence beyond their follows, comments, and likes. The numbers don't lie. A big follower count doesn't really mean high engagement, and a smaller follower count won't always mean less engagement statistics.

3.  A few things to consider: Since you are telling this person to represent your brand or be a spokesperson for a given period of time, you need to consider how they will capture your brand voice while keeping it personal to their brand. This is because how new customers perceive your brand through this person is what they would associate you with. If the voice captured is calm and collected, consumers will expect a similar experience on your page. If it is hyped and over the top, they will expect the same, too. You should also make sure to work on brand alignment by ensuring the person you are working with understands enough about

who you are to effectively sell your brand, especially in uncontrolled environments like Instagram Lives where you don't have a second take and can't filter things out.

4. Create a strategy: You want to have guidelines on what will be the contributions toward either party, what your expectations are, and how you are going to make sure they are met. Strategies are always good to clarify the job each party will have to contribute to your goals, and the expectations they need to raise to.

**How to Use UGC**

- Always ask for permission.

Even after someone has used the directed guidelines you shared, like your brand hashtags, or tagged you, you should still ask for their permission to use their images. It is first of all a legal requirement to ask a user to use their likeness for your brand, and it's a courtesy to ask someone if you could use their content to share your message. Something as simple as reaching out to them via DMs or their comment section under their image goes a long way.

- Credit the owner.

Beyond asking for permission, always credit the owner of the image, video, or other content types. Always tag their handle in the image or in the comment section.

It's a way to drive traffic to your page, and also give free exposure to them, which makes it a win-win situation on both ends. Some brands would opt to go for the original caption used by the creator on their content to leave a touch of authenticity, or create a whole new one that drives the message they are trying to put out. It's up to you to decide what will best suit your brand objectives.

- Make it relevant.

If your users are looking for winter shoes and jackets, as a brand selling clothes it makes no sense to share your summer section full of bikinis and flip-flops. Align it with what your users are looking for and share the correspondent content accordingly. If you study your user habits long enough, you'll know how seasons influence their needs and which products or services are needed the most. This will help you better align any shared UGC according to demand. Studying consumer behaviors and buying decisions is paramount as demand shifts numerous times a year.

- Make it accessible.

Instagram enables creators or business accounts to include a catalog or make their posts shoppable, which makes your products more accessible. This makes it easy for users to make a buying decision, or reduce the number of times you'll receive repeated comments and DMs asking how much something is and how they can access it.

**Step 5:**

# The Power of Hashtags

Instagram hashtags are used to group and filter content within a specific niche or topic to make it more discoverable. Users utilize hashtags to find the exact kind of content they are looking for, which makes it the best way to increase organic impressions of your brand content and brand visibility. Using hashtags can be tricky, but done right, it could elevate your content and brand exponentially. On the flip side, if used wrong, they will affect your posts and potentially have your content flagged as spam by the Instagram algorithms, which affects how you show up in front of Instagram users.

Should you use hashtags for every post you make? The answer is yes. Here are a few reasons why:

- Improve your organic reach: When you hashtag your post, it goes from being shown to your followers to the broader market of people looking at content similar to yours. This, in turn, increases the number of people viewing your content and could potentially help you reach new followers and grow your community.

- Increase engagement and visibility: The higher your reach, the higher the number of people interacting with your content. Some who view your content might not follow you immediately, but if what you posted stood out enough for them, they could like, comment, or even save your post, which increases your brand engagement and visibility. It also works in your favor with the algorithms.

- Generate interest: Numerous people follow at least one hashtag on Instagram, which means the possibility of someone who doesn't follow you seeing your post is increased by at least 50% with a hashtag. You can generate user interest by creating eye-catching and relevant content, which possibly leads to a follow, save, or share, which benefits and boosts your brand visibility.

## Best Case Practices to Use Hashtags

Instagram allows as many as 30 hashtags on a single post. Some would go crazy with using all 30 on every post, while others would limit it to as low as one. As a content creator, you can use any number between one and thirty (even none). However, Instagram recommends that creators use at least three to five hashtags per post. Remember that your hashtag game can make or break your content reach to a broader audience. And since you want to keep growing your page regardless of how many followers you have, here are the best case practices for using hashtags:

- Keep it relevant: If you sell makeup, don't use hashtags that travel companies would use, or if you provide car rental services, it wouldn't be relevant for you to use a hashtag that is specific to foodies and food bloggers. Your post will be disconnected from the collective group of posts under that hashtag and make you stand out for the wrong reasons. Make your hashtags relevant by using niche-specific hashtags, language that people in your niche would use, a word or phrase that is most likely to come up in the industry, or something specific to the post you are making. Examples of a food blogger hashtag would be #foodie, #food, #foodphotography, and #photooftheday. These hashtags group the user as a food blogger; they group them among posts showcasing food and photos of the day to showcase their photography skills. This, in essence, has put you in front of people looking at food images and people admiring beautiful photography and photography angles: two separate communities.

- Balance out the number of hashtags: Using all 30 hashtags for every post could bulk your caption and make your content look like spam. On the other hand, using too few hashtags limits the number of people you can reach. Keep in mind that you have numerous other content creators you are competing with for user attention on a daily basis. You can keep your caption looking clean by limiting the number of hashtags to at least three to five carefully targeted and curated hashtags, or use other tricks if you feel you absolutely must use all 30. Some prefer to post them in the comment section, so they are entirely out of the caption, while others create at least four to five paragraphs and input the hashtags so they are hidden further down from the caption. Either way, try to not use all 30 hashtags on your posts as much as possible. Many people find it off-putting to interact with content riddled with hashtags. Numerous hashtags also drown out your captions, which is not good for your content.

- Avoid banned hashtags: A hashtag gets banned from Instagram when the content under it is reported enough times. This is when content posted under it is deemed inappropriate or goes against content guidelines. Some of these hashtags are very unassuming and you would think it was okay to use them, for example,

#always or #brain. Never assume that it is okay to use a hashtag simply because it seems harmless. Curate a list of hashtags you will be using for your posts on your content calendar, then go through each of them and make sure it's not a banned hashtag. You can cross-check with numerous online websites that work on keeping track of banned hashtags for fast work. Ideally, you can go through Instagram only to check out the quality posts posted under the hashtags you are going for.

- Use saturated hashtags sparingly: Saturated hashtags are those with a million-plus posts. These hashtags are being used by many users, which means your content is likely to get drowned in this hashtag the second you post it. Using all saturated hashtags in your posts means the possibility of your content ranking higher in the hashtags list is decreased tenfold. Just because multiple people are using a hashtag doesn't mean you should jump on that bandwagon, too. On the other hand, hashtags with a 10,000 count and under mean that there is not much engagement with those particular hashtags. You can find a good balance using one or two saturated hashtags (as long as they are relevant), and then the other number(s), however many you choose, can be within the range of 10,000-plus to no more than a million.

- Avoid vague hashtags: Hashtags like #beauty are a lot less informative than #beautybloggers (P.S. #beautyblogger is a banned hashtag. Note the missing 's' here). Anything can fall under #beauty, and yet #beautybloggers specifies exactly what kind of content a user will find under that particular hashtag. Vague hashtags are generally broad enough words to cover a wide range of topics and don't narrow down your content to what it is. They are also less likely to be searched for by users. An example of vague hashtags are #good, #ice, #now, and #here, versus more specific hashtags like #icecream, #photodump, and #healingbathsalts. Drowning your content with vague hashtags will only hurt your marketing efforts.

## *Hashtags Curation Steps*

- Research.

Researching hashtags is simplified on Instagram. With just one word in the search bar, you are given a list of similar hashtags under the Tags bar, with the number of posts under it to know how active that hashtag is. You can decide to write down the numerous hashtags you feel relates to your brand and what core message you want to pass to your audience. Keep inputting different brand-related words in the search bar to get different hashtag ideas. Another way to compile a list of hashtags is to go through brands in your niche and check the hashtags they use the most. Balance it out between different kinds of businesses, like small businesses, big brands, individuals or groups, etc. Write down the hashtags that appear repeatedly, plus keep an eye out for how they use their hashtags (in terms of placement, number of hashtags, and the message in the image or video versus the corresponding hashtag).

- Check out the content under each hashtag.

While this step can easily be done during the research stage, it helps to simply focus on creating your hashtags list before you dig deeper. This helps keep your mind clear and focused as digging under each hashtag requires you to look out for different things. It's also much faster to find a list first, then work through the list, choosing which hashtags you will use and which ones you will discard. When you have your list of niche hashtags, carefully go through one hashtag at a time scrolling as deep as you can to decide if you want to be grouped with content under that particular hashtag. You want to first go through the Top tab to understand how the interactions on the top posts look. Then, through the Recent tab, get an idea of how often posts appear under that hashtag and the kind of content being posted daily. You can refresh your page to see if there are any new posts and get an idea of how active that hashtag is. The Reels section is important if you plan on doing Reels, and it's basically the same idea as before. Checking content under a specific hashtag is a good way to create a list of niche hashtags you want to stay away from as much as the ones you'll be using.

- Create your unique hashtag.

If you are looking at growing your community, unique hashtags will go a long way for you. They help you and your content stand out by grouping any posts that use that hashtag as one, similar to how the broad hashtags would work. Unique hashtags help you control the conversations surrounding your brand when your users use your brand hashtag, making it easy to find and engage with user-generated content. To create your own hashtag, first, think about the kind of message you want to drive by using that hashtag. Do you want to engage your community, drive a campaign, or group your services? Whichever one it is, find something that will speak to your objective. If you want to engage your community, you can decide to turn your community name into a hashtag and encourage others in your community to do the same. However, before you decide on your final hashtag, be sure to cross-check that it isn't a banned hashtag or doesn't have tones that might be misinterpreted, like the infamous #susanalbumparty.

- Think about your content pillars.

Your list of content pillars is a great guide to the kind of hashtags you should be on the lookout for. Find hashtags that you want to use, then group your core hashtags into the different content pillars that they will be falling under. You will not be using the same hashtags for every post, nor for every content pillar. This will be a good way to help you group and easily find what will fall under what. There are, of course, some core hashtags that will show up for each post, like your unique hashtag, but not every hashtag you have will be relevant to every post you make. Keep that in mind when working on your content calendar.

- Keep it relevant.

If you are a food brand, keep your hashtags relevant to food. If you are a clothes company, keep your hashtags relevant to clothes. It might be tempting to keep a hashtag you see used by similar brands, but if it's not relevant to yours, it shouldn't be on your list. People who search for hashtags instead of scrolling through posts on their timeline do so because they are looking for something very specific. If what you are posting is not relevant to that hashtag, it only hurts your chances of finding a wider community.

- Use local hashtags.

Local hashtags are those that group your post into a given location. These won't showcase specific and similar content, but rather content being posted by people and brands in your area. They are a good way to get discovered locally, so don't shy away from using these tags. They are curated the same way that brand hashtags are, but be sure to find which one you want to use. With location hashtags, they are always the same, but could have one difference at the end; for example, #london versus #londoncity. It can also be popular lingo in your local area that locals will immediately understand, or a name that only locals call their city, etc.

# Chapter 6:

# Instagram and the Visual Influence

Instagram's visual platform makes it important to create the most compelling images and videos as the images speak for your brand before anything else. People judge your brand based on what you have posted before they read any captions you use to try and convince them to buy or interact with you. Your Instagram page is like one endlessly running marketing campaign that will either draw in a following or chase people away, never mind how great your content is or how clever your captions are.

Part of what makes Instagram the fastest growing platform is the fact that it depends on visuals to give a message, making it accessible to everyone, regardless of the fact that they speak your language or not. This is why you need to put a lot of focus and invest the best in creating compelling visuals for your Instagram page.

# Rules of a Visually Pleasing Instagram Page

1. Showcase your brand personality:

Your brand personality is your brand colors, fonts, and even specific shapes. Your brand personality will speak for you before you say anything, and could potentially compel people to look deeper than the surface into your page. Colors, fonts, and shapes all tell stories and are a good way for you to create a compelling page feed. You can also play around with them to showcase your brand personality, like in videos, Stories, and Reels. It's all about exploring to find what works for you.

2. Clean photography:

Photography is an essential part of your marketing strategy as it's what will help you bring your brand personality to life. Clean photography is basically having images where the subject stands out, great light-shadow balance, compelling tones, texture, etc. Clean photographs make for a clean-looking and compelling page. It's a good way to showcase your brand personality with colors and textures to give different depth to your content. It's good to keep backgrounds, angles, and perspectives in mind, and to ensure that featured items fit within your brand personality in terms of colors, shapes, and layouts.

3. Plan ahead:

One thing about creating something beautiful and compelling is actually planning ahead. Planning helps you better understand how each image or video you take will look like, what objects or items you will need to have at hand, and generally make your work easier when making the content you need. Planning ahead also helps you create bulk content which saves you time and allows you to focus on one different stage of creating a post on Instagram at a time.

4. Keep it consistent:

Consistency is when you keep your page's same look that sets your brand apart from the others. It can also be as simple as using the same filter for every post (if you use filters) or adding the same kinds of tones and textures in any editing software you use outside Instagram's provided filters. Consistency comes in product placement (flat lays or close-ups), how you play around with your brand colors, and the perspective in your images, among others. Beyond the visuals, your tone should also stay consistent to your brand for every post you make.

5. Show people:

While it's good to showcase your products and services, it's more important that you add a humane element to your page. People buy from people, and knowing that beyond that beautiful bottle of lotion is a real person brings a more humane touch to your content. It also is a great way to create a connection between you and your followers, as they get the opportunity to associate a face to a product or service they may grow fond of.

## *Engagement Tips on Instagram*

Now you have your visually compelling feed ready to put out, or you have already launched. The most important thing you want to do now is build engagement. You have put the work in to create something your followers would appreciate, and now it's important to find the people that will come check out your content. As with everything that involves execution, you need to plan ahead on how you will do that. The following tips give an idea of how you can boost engagement on your Instagram page.

1. The $1.80 Strategy

Entrepreneur Gary Vaynerchuk created this strategy for engagement on Instagram. The idea behind this strategy is to boost engagement and grow your community by putting yourself where your potential community is, getting involved with like-minded people and brands, and leaving a worthwhile mark wherever you want to appear. The premise is quite simple: Find the 10 trending hashtags in your niche for the day, and leave a comment on the top nine posts under all of the 10 hashtags. This way you have left your .02 cents, which translates to $1.80 worth of comments left under 90 posts. The comment you leave should add value and push the relevant conversation, whether it's something serious to contribute more to the conversation, leaving an insightful comment, or merely being funny. Generally go for a comment that will get positive reactions from the readers. Avoid comments that won't leave the right impression, like unnecessary self-promotion and being unnecessarily negative under someone's comment section. Find a good balance between commenting on top posts and recent posts, aiming for those posted within the day.

2. Engage your community

There are numerous ways you can engage your community, or engage *with* them. You can engage your community with Story stickers where you get to ask questions, recommendations, their opinions, or generally anything fun you can think of that will get people talking. You can also run a weekly series that they can look forward to like Lives, or produce a specific kind of content on specific days. You can engage with your community by responding to any messages or comments that they leave you, or going as far as checking out their profiles and engaging with their posts that have nothing to do with your brand or content.

3. Create shareable posts

From relatable memes, informative carousels, funny Reels, and anything in between, there are plenty of ways you can make your content worth a share. The three principles of engaging content are "Educate, Entertain and Excite." Create your content with these three principles in mind. As mentioned earlier, you can take one idea and create three different posts from it that fit into these principles. This generally ensures that you always have something to say. You can also utilize the Highlights feature, which helps you keep your Stories active on your page even when they're no longer active as a Story.

4. Include calls to action

Take this as what you'd want your audience to do with your post. So you took an amazing photo of your shoe, so what? Calls to action are a kind of guidance to people letting them know what you want from them in terms of the content you shared. Do you want them to navigate to the link in bio for more? Leave their opinions? Share their similar stories? Tag a friend? What do you want your users to do with what you've shared with them?

5. Encourage collabs

Instagram Reels gives an opportunity for anyone to remix your Reel and turn it into their own. The more this happens, the more people you reach as your content is shared more. You can also utilize your brand hashtags to encourage more of your audience to use them for their content.

**Step 7:**

# Grow With Your Metrics

Also called insights or analytics, Instagram metrics are insights into your content performance and are available to every creator or business page. Insights give you information about your page that goes beyond the surface of how many likes you receive. Any and all content posted on Instagram will be tracked, whether it's Stories, Reels, or posts, making it easy for you to track your brand's growth (or lack thereof). It's important to keep up-to-date with your metrics because it will help you elevate your page and your brand.

With metrics, you can:

- Track how your community is growing.

Instagram tracks the number of new follows and unfollows for you, which gives you an idea of overall growth. It also goes in-depth to show you which posts had people follow and unfollow your account, which is an invaluable way of knowing what kind of posts work for you or against you.

- Learn more about your posts' performance.

Beyond likes and comments, the metrics will let you know how many times your posts were seen (impressions), how many unique accounts your posts reached (reach), how many people visited your account, how many accounts engaged with you, how many actions were taken while on your page—like ask for directions, check out website, etc. (interactions)—and how many times your handle was mentioned. This can all be tracked in a given period of time; for example, weekly or monthly, and up to 90 days.

- Keep on top of your follower demographics.

The location of your followers can be grouped into cities and countries to show you where the highest percentage of your followers is from, down to the lowest percentage. It will also show you the age range of your followers, and you can decide to group it into only men or women or view both gender percentages. The same goes for the gender of men versus women who are following you.

- Track content performance.

You will be provided with the opportunity to see which of your posted content types drives the most engagement (Reels, photos, videos), and break it down further to individual posts to understand your post performance.

- Create a better content strategy.

The information provided by the insights gives you a better idea of who your audience is, when they are most active daily, what posts get the most engagement from your followers, etc. This will help you adjust your content strategy and design what kind of content your followers are looking for. The metrics also provide you an idea of what kind of content is your highest-performing, which is knowledge you can use to create more of that content.

# How To Use Metrics To Grow

In order to get the most out of your metrics, you need to be informed about what it is you are looking for out of your content performance, so you have a clear understanding of what you are tracking.

- What is important to you?

Is it more important for you to have impressions or a wider reach? Is it more important to have more followers or more people visiting your website? Are you interested in creating a leads magnet? To be able to use your metrics to inform your decisions, you need to, first of all, decide what exactly is important to you and then which of the provided metrics will help you track it. This part makes defining the rest of your metric analysis easy.

- Identify your top performers.

Top performing content helps you know which kind of content resonates the best with your audience. Instagram insights can group it for you in terms of the content types or by telling you what individual post under which content type performed the best. You can find out how each photo performed, for example, and what kind of actions were taken under each photo (like clicking the call button, email, follow, etc.). This can be done for all your posts and gives you the opportunity to group your most interacted with content to inform how your content calendar will look like.

- Post when your followers are live.

The metrics also provide a breakdown of the time your followers use Instagram. They break it down further to how many people were online at what hour of the day throughout the week. These insights are highly useful, especially with the customized feeds as they provide you an idea of at what time of the day you should post and the days your following is the most active.

## *The Don'ts of Growing on Instagram*

While we all want to grow fast on Instagram, there are some practices you should stay far away from. Instagram has great power to elevate or hurt your brand based on how your use the platform, which is why you should take care to avoid the following:

- Buying followers: It's tempting to try to raise the number of followers in a short period of time, but bought followers are nothing but bot accounts. Not only do these not engage, but they also hurt your chances of showing up under real accounts as they add zero value to you. This is why you'll often find accounts with thousands of followers, with only 10 likes and at most one comment. And while we are on the subject, stay away from buying likes and comments, too. Invest your time and energy in organically harnessing real people and real engagement for a better idea of how your content is really performing. It's better to invest your money in running ads than it is in buying followers, because ads will help you grow exactly where you want to grow.

- Spamming: Instagram has limits to the number of things you can do within the same period, like following new accounts or sending DMs. Your activity can get limited if you consistently perform the same action within a limited amount of time, like copying and pasting the same message from inbox to inbox or to different comment sections. You might potentially get flagged as a spam account, too, due to suspicious behavior. Spamming can also be when you constantly post comments that serve no purpose to the post at hand. While it might not be flagged as spam from Instagram itself, it will be recognized and labeled as spam from Instagram users who see your comment.

- Selling in every post: You don't have to slap the "buy from me" sign in your audience's face with every post you make. If people want to buy from you, they will; if they don't want to, they won't. If you've ever been heckled by a salesperson while you were busy minding your business on the streets, then you definitely know the feeling of having something shoved in front of you when you didn't ask for it. Aim to provide value to your customers instead by showcasing your product or service at work, and then let them decide if they still want to buy or not. A good way to balance out sales posts is aiming for 20% of your posts to be about buying from you, and 80% about providing value to your potential client.

- Not responding to your audience: Sure, you're busy, and maybe you could have one too many comments to respond to, but taking the initiative to respond to as many comments as you can showcases to your followers that you are interested in engaging with them and value the time they take to leave that comment. A lack of response on all comments is louder than a response on a few comments.

- Posting negative comments: As with any business that deals with customer care, you will find a great deal of rude and negative people both in your comments section and your DMs. While it is tempting to respond back with the same energy you receive, all it will do is hurt you and your business. A negative comment never really goes away for you. If you don't think you'll be able to respond to something positively, it's okay to leave it as it is and move on; if it's unavoidable that you send a response, take a walk away from that message, then come back to it when levelheaded.

- Poor quality images or content: This is a major reason why you absolutely must create a content calendar and plan for your posts ahead of time. One poor quality post is excusable. More than one is off-putting. Find the right equipment and the right resources to give your customers and followers the value they deserve, then actually make your content mean something.

- Post and ghost: Just because you are posting something doesn't mean the work is done. Instagram strives for engagement, and as someone seeking engagement on your posts, you have to actually be engaged on the platform. The $1.80 Strategy is a good way to engage when you don't know where to start. Another trick you can do to boost engagement on your posts is engaging for a maximum of 30 minutes before you post on your page, then engaging some more for 30 minutes on different pages and posts after posting to drive traffic to your page. Always balance out your engagement with posts that have great engagement and those with low engagement.

# Conclusion

Gone are the days when you had to run Yellow Pages and TV ads to be able to reach your audience. Today, social media has made reaching audiences very quick and easy, providing faster results and the means to track these results to help you have a deeper understanding of customer behavior.

Even then, the job doesn't end with making a post. Working on Instagram is a never-ending innovation project, where you need to learn to tweak your posts, captions, and even your profile bio every now and then to fit your ever-growing audience and changing business needs.

If you want to maintain a high-ranking profile that converts results, you need to be able to keep up with your competition and your community needs. This is especially through keeping up with a few nonnegotiables that must be added to your monthly to-do list.

- Keep up with Instagram.

Instagram is ever-changing and ever-growing to keep up with its growing users and user needs. Make it your mission to keep up with any new features and what they mean for you as a business on Instagram. Check out the official Instagram pages for businesses and creators for any news that might affect you, and use the numerous resources available to grow your page. Instagram wants everyone who uses its platform to grow and use the platform to the maximum. It does this by providing the information they think will be useful to you.

- Review your content and insights.

This should become a habit for you. Carve out some time monthly to review your content, go through your metrics, and find your best performers to help you understand what drives the most conversions for you. It's important to do it monthly because that provides enough time for your content to circulate to have useful numbers you can use to inform your future decisions. Don't be afraid to adjust with your metrics.

- Change with your community.

As your community grows, so should you. Give your community what they want by giving them more of the content they want, while also allowing yourself to keep true to your brand and where you started from. While the changes don't have to be drastic, it's nice to show your community that you hear them and care about their needs.

- Keep up with your community.

Engage with other brands, create exciting opportunities to engage with your community, check out what others in your niche are talking about and what you can contribute to the conversation, and check out what your community is sharing and how you can react (this is something you should do daily). These little habits help you keep on top of the algorithms.

- Review the community guidelines at least once.

Read the fine print! Instagram is very particular about the kind of content they want and don't want on its platform, and vigilantly works to keep its community safe. Ensure that you review the community guidelines at least once to understand what is expected of you as a content creator and business owner on the platform.

- Avoid shadow-banning at all costs.

When an account gets shadow-banned by Instagram, it means that the account is not viewed by anyone besides the people that follow you, no matter if you use hashtags and similar other tricks that get you to a wider audience. Shadow-banning happens when you use too many irrelevant hashtags, constantly violate community guidelines, use harmful practices like buying followers, and use banned hashtags consistently, among other practices.

Using Instagram is a fun way to showcase your brand. You are in full control of how your brand is perceived. Take that knowledge and showcase your brand just how you want your followers and the community you are growing to see you!

# References

Ademola Abimbola. (2017, February 21). *The Role of Social Media in Decision Making*. Mauco Enterprises. https://mauconline.net/the-role-of-social-media-in-decision-making/

Alexandra. (2022, March 12). *List of All the Instagram New Features & Updates (in 2022)*. Preview App. https://thepreviewapp.com/instagram-new-features-2022/

Bagadiya, J. (2022, March). *9 Instagram Business Marketing Mistakes You Should Avoid*. Www.socialpilot.co. https://www.socialpilot.co/blog/9-instagram-business-marketing-mistakes-avoid

Business Victoria. (2021, March 9). *Define and know your customer*. Business Victoria. https://business.vic.gov.au/business-information/marketing-and-sales/increasing-sales-through-marketing/define-and-know-your-customer#:~:text=Creating%20a%20customer%20profile%20or%20persona

, J. (2022, January 24). *Instagram Creator vs Business Account.* Synchedin Blog. https://synchedin.com/blog/instagram-creator-vs-business-account/

Carbone, L. (2020, March 4). *Should You Switch to an Instagram Creator Profile?* Later.com. https://later.com/blog/instagram-creator-profile/#worth

Chron Contributor. (2020, September 8). *Why I always use TurboTax to do my own taxes.* Small Business - Chron.com. https://smallbusiness.chron.com/turbotax-taxes-13771756.html

Cooper, P. (2019, July 2). *How the Instagram Algorithm Works in 2019 (And How to Work With It).* Hootsuite Social Media Management. https://blog.hootsuite.com/instagram-algorithm/

Daugherty, J. (2021, June 14). *Content Pillar Examples.* Www.demandjump.com. https://www.demandjump.com/blog/content-pillar-examples

Donawerth, S. (2020, February 6). *Instagram Creator vs Business Account - What's the Difference?* Carro: Sell More, Together.

https://getcarro.com/blog/instagram-creator-vs-business-account/#:~:text=Business%20and%20Creator%20accounts%20have

Dreghorn, B. (2020, April 6). *What is the Difference Between the 3 Instagram Profile Types*. Business 2 Community. https://www.business2community.com/instagram/what-is-the-difference-between-the-3-instagram-profile-types-02300390

Fenberg, J. (2020, March 9). *7 Steps for Building an Online Community + 5 Examples*. The BigCommerce Blog. https://www.bigcommerce.com/blog/online-communities/#7-steps-for-building-an-online-community

Geyser, W. (2022, February 22). *How to Post on Instagram in 2022: The Ultimate Guide*. Influencer Marketing Hub. https://influencermarketinghub.com/how-to-post-on-instagram/#toc-2

Golob, L. (2022, January 5). *Instagram tests three new options for how posts appear in user feeds*. Social Media Marketing & Management Dashboard. https://blog.hootsuite.com/social-media-updates/instagram/instagram-tests-new-feeds/

S. (2021, October 8). *Instagram Collaboration: Benefits of Collaborating with Instagram Influencers.* Influence4You - Agence et Plateforme D'influence. https://blogen.influence4you.com/instagram-collaboration-benefits-of-collaborating-with-instagram-influencers/#:~:text=Instagram%20collaboration%20is%20an%20excellent

Holloway, H. (2021, June 1). *How Social Media Marketing Is Positively Changing The Business World - Eclincher.* Eclincher. https://eclincher.com/how-social-media-marketing-is-changing-business/#:~:text=It

*How to Be Authentic on Instagram.* (n.d.). WikiHow. Retrieved April 17, 2022, from https://www.wikihow.com/Be-Authentic-on-Instagram

Huynh, J. (2021, March 11). *How to perform an Instagram competitor analysis [template included].* Supermetrics. https://supermetrics.com/blog/instagram-competitor-analysis

Instagram. (n.d.-a). *Engage with Your Community with Instagram Stories.* Instagram for Creators. Retrieved April 23, 2022, from https://creators.instagram.com/stories

Instagram. (n.d.-b). *Instagram Reels: Create and discover short videos on Instagram*. Instagram for Business. https://business.instagram.com/instagram-reels

IZEA. (2018, November 29). *Influencer Marketing Business Model*. IZEA. https://izea.com/resources/influencer-marketing-business-model-2/#:~:text=The%20influencer%20marketing%20business%20model

Johnston, M. (2021, January 22). *Instagram Creator vs Business account: Which is right for you?* Vamp. https://vamp-brands.com/blog/2021/01/22/instagram-creator-vs-business-account-which-is-right-for-you/#:~:text=Instagram%20suggests%20that%20the%20Creator

Kennedy, J. (2017, February 28). *5 Interesting Pillars of The Marketing Strategy - ProcurementExpress.com*. ProcurementExpress.com. https://www.procurementexpress.com/marketing/marketing-strategy/

Keyhole. (2019, July 22). *Instagram Creator Account: Is It Worth The Switch?* Keyhole. https://keyhole.co/blog/instagram-creator-account/

.20, April 20). *How Do I Calculate Engagement Rate?* Keyhole. https://keyhole.co/blog/how-do-i-calculate-engagement-rate/#what

Later: The All-In-One Social Marketing Platform. (2020, September 25). *How to Build a Community on Instagram.* Www.youtube.com. [Video]. https://www.youtube.com/watch?v=as6loKuK f5c

Le, J. (2021, January 19). *How To Create Your Own Hashtag (and Why You'd Want To).* Spark Growth. https://sparkgrowth.com/hashtag/#:~:text=W hy%20should%20you%20create%20a

Lockerbie, A. (2020, September 25). *What is User Generated Content (And How to Use it for Your Business).* Www.youtube.com. [Video] https://www.youtube.com/watch?v=roNWFxr YYBI&t=438s

Martin, M. (2022, March 23). *Instagram Monetization: A Complete Guide for Creators and Influencers.* Social Media Marketing & Management Dashboard. https://blog.hootsuite.com/instagram-monetization/

Mowbray-Allen, K. (2020, July 1). *The Pros and Cons of Facebook's New Feature: Creator Studio.* Hellomedia.

https://www.hellomedia.team/blogs/blog/the-pros-and-cons-of-facebook-new-feature-creator-studio

Neal, J. L. (2022, January 1). *The Definitive Guide to the Instagram Creator Studio in 2022 | Informative Speech Topics.* Informative Speech Topics. https://informativespeechtopics.org/instagram-creator-studio/

Neeraj. (2019, April 25). *User Generated Content Marketing & Its Unavoidable Benefits.* Taggbox Blog. https://taggbox.com/blog/user-generated-content/

Nevue, D. (2022, January 21). *5 Reasons Why Your Instagram Hashtags Are Not Working.* Nevue Fine Art Marketing. https://www.nevuefineartmarketing.com/5-reasons-why-your-instagram-hashtags-are-not-working/

Newberry, C. (2019, February 7). *The 2019 Instagram Hashtag Guide—How to Use Them and Get Results.* Hootsuite Social Media Management. https://blog.hootsuite.com/instagram-hashtags/

Newman, C. (2017). *What is a Value Proposition? (Plus 3 Great Examples and 3 Common Mistakes).*

ocreative.com.
https://www.kunocreative.com/blog/good-value-proposition-examples

Ordonio, C. (2017, December 15). *Instagram Hashtag Do's and Don'ts*. Reader Digital Agency. https://www.readerdigital.com/instagram-hashtag-dos-and-donts/

Polishchuk, D. (2021, September 28). *What Is a Good Instagram Engagement Rate in 2021?* PromoRepublic. https://promorepublic.com/en/blog/what-is-a-good-instagram-engagement-rate-in-2021/

Puntschart, L. (2021, July 8). *Educate, entertain, engage & inspire — Part 02 A step by step guide*. Medium. https://lindapuntschart.medium.com/educate-entertain-engage-inspire-part-02-a-step-by-step-guide-31950b0cda72

Reba, M. (2021). *What Does Instagram Interactions Mean? – The Nina*. Www.thenina.com. https://www.thenina.com/what-does-instagram-interactions-mean/#1

Routley, N. (2017, November 17). *The Influence of Instagram*. Visual Capitalist. https://www.visualcapitalist.com/influence-of-instagram/

Singal, N. (2020, February 28). *User-Generated Content Marketing: Organic Tactics To Grow Brand Trust & Sales.* Www.linkedin.com. https://www.linkedin.com/pulse/user-generated-content-marketing-organic-tactics-grow-neeraj-singal

Taylor, N. (2015, June 12). *Why Are #Hashtags So Darn Important?* Association Adviser. https://www.naylor.com/associationadviser/why-are-hashtags-important/

Thomas, M. (2020, November 5). *How to Use Content Pillars for Social Media.* Later Blog. https://later.com/blog/content-pillars-for-social-media/

Thomas, M. (2021, October 20). *Everything You Need to Know About Instagram Collabs.* Later.com. https://later.com/blog/instagram-collabs/

Ugbaja, L. (2021, August 20). *Instagram Mistakes: 7 Things to Avoid Posting on Instagram As a Business in 2021 | Databox Blog.* Databox. https://databox.com/instagram-posting-mistakes

Vaynerchuk, G. (785 C.E., April 9). *The $1.80 Instagram Strategy To Grow Your Business or Brand.* GaryVaynerchuk.com.

ps://www.garyvaynerchuk.com/instagram-for-business-180-strategy-grow-business-brand/

arren, J. (2019a, January 30). *Instagram Hashtags: The Ultimate Guide (2019 Update)*. Later Blog. https://later.com/blog/ultimate-guide-to-using-instagram-hashtags/

Warren, J. (2019b, June 7). *This is How The Instagram Algorithm Works in 2019*. Later Blog. https://later.com/blog/how-instagram-algorithm-works/

Whitney, M. (2021, November 25). *The Complete Guide to Instagram Analytics*. Www.wordstream.com. https://www.wordstream.com/blog/ws/2018/11/01/instagram-analytics

Worb, J. (2019, January 27). *9 Ways to Increase Instagram Engagement in 2019 - Later Blog*. Later Blog. https://later.com/blog/how-to-increase-instagram-engagement/

Printed in Great Britain
by Amazon

29196991R00056